AF426704

Bits And Pieces Of Me

by
Randy Hayes

This manuscript was developed in the Kern River
Valley Art Association Poetry Workshop with
Sandra Hughes
and John Peterson

Poetic Matrix Press
www.poeticmatrix.com

Content

Dedication

Randy Hayes (Bio)

Dedication

*To the People of
the Kern River Valley*

Time For Everything

He described her as delicious.
He watched her from afar.
He said that he had time.
Until she died in that car.

There is time for everything.
Until that time runs out.
Until the end intervenes.
Now it's something to cry about.

I once knew a young man.
Who waited to cash out.
When he showed up at the window.
The bottom had fallen out.

He got not one penny.
Till the court was done.
Then he got a fraction.
He was not the only one.

She waited to have babies.
Until she was too old.
She partied it away.
That's how her time was sold.

She told her husband "Next year."
Every time that he would try.
Until the operation.
Now all she does is cry.

There is time for everything.
Of the excuses be aware.
If your time is tied to someone else.
Take the time to share.

Fortune

A fortune means nothing.
With no one to share.
Living a life.
With no reason to care.

A heart needs someone.
To love and to hold.
Love is a fortune.
More precious than gold.

There are some people.
Six feet below (the) ground.
When they went away.
There was not one weeping sound.

They left a treasure.
To relatives never met.
They left it behind.
They lost that bet.

Toad

I see something green.
Crossing the road.
I dart to the right.
It's a great big green toad.

Up the embankment.
Then back down again.
Back on the road.
Where I start to spin.

The people behind me.
Must think I'm insane.
But that big ole toad.
Is safe again.

Golden

Some days are golden.
Some days are tin.
Some days you lose.
Some days you win.

Sometimes your gold.
Shines in the sky.
Some days are silver.
Clouds don't ever ask why.

Some days are wet.
Tinged with tears.
They help you to reach.
Your golden years.

Keeping And Saving

I've been keeping and saving.
Dang near all my life.
I still have the first thing.
That I gave my loving wife.

It's a box without the candy.
Because she ate it all.
I even saved the wrapping.
Yes sir, I saved it all.

In a drawer I have the baseball glove.
That I was given as a boy.
And my first baseball too.
They filled my heart with joy.

My first bicycle.
Is hanging in my garage,
Right over my first car.
A 1950 Dodge.

Would you like to see the paper?
From my first candy bar?
It's over there with the others.
In that great big pickle jar.

I'd offer you a place to sit.
But the house is overrun.
With 50 years of collecting.
And it's been a lot of fun.

Turning Tides

I can feel the tides are turning.
I see the waves come in.
The directions are shifting.
As I take it on the chin.

I have walked upon this earth
Since the day I pulled me up.
It's the way that children learn.
If adults don't interrupt.

Memories of the mundane.
Simply flushed from my head.
I don't choose to remember them.
They might as well be dead.

Here I sit retired.
My swollen fingers hurt.
That was one tide that turned.
Mother Nature is a flirt.

I always thought I'd play guitar.
And write life changing tunes.
My guitar sits there against the wall.
My joints swelled like balloons.

I write a lot of poetry.
Some people like them a lot.
That's a tide that just rolled in.
A gift that I never bought.

I can feel the tides wash over me.
A new direction for my soul.
I'll take it with a humble smile.
As the tides take control.

Living In The Future

I got up this morning.
Only what did I find?
That time had passed by.
Was leaving me behind.

Everything I do.
Everything I did.
Is now in my past.
Even before I was a kid.

Every second comes and goes.
There is no further can't you see?
The present is so fleeting.
That even it can never be.

When people talk about the future.
It brings me to tears.
Because the only place that exists.
Is between their ears.

Migrations

I've been noticing migrations.
Maybe you have too.
I especially notice them.
With every shampoo.

I have to clean the drain.
Of tons of my hair.
I should card and spin it.
Then weave it up with care.

I can see the migration.
Of my receding young hairline.
All of those wrinkles.
Even the ones that are looking fine.

The migration of my jowls.
Drooping of my chin.
My soft and veiny legs.
It should be a sin.

Now that I have the time.
The migrations multiply.
They tell me it's old age.
And there ain't no need to cry.

My teeth are leaving day by day.
And as they migrate away?
I can only shake my head.
And hope that a few of them will stay.

Fire Born

She was born amongst the fire.
Sheltered from the flames.
People came to rescue her.
She will never know their names.

They wrapped her in a blanket.
As the roof came crashing down.
They took her and her momma.
To much safer ground.

Her mother named her Ember.
She has flaming frizzed red hair.
She wears a locket filled with ashes.
That her mother gathered for her with care.

One night I saw her dancing.
As flames ruled the night.
She smiled as she raised her arms.
"Don't you think I've earned the right?"

She whirled and twirled and laughed out loud.
A chill shot up my spine.
I swear I saw some dragons.
Standing in a line.

When the flames had left the land.
She returned to her happy ways.
But in my mind the thing I saw.
Stays with me for always.

She got herself a big tattoo.
Of a dragon spewing flame.
She named him, "Puff The Magic."
She said she loves that name.

Today's Weather

Today's weather is filled with smoke.
I can't see the sky.
They tell me to just relax.
It's not my time to die.

The bright red of the cinders.
Rain down upon the earth.
Next time they say it rains.
The plants will have (a) rebirth.

As the trees ignite in flames.
Here I stand with garden hose.
There I see a fire a devil.
A tornado I suppose.

A plane flies low there overhead.
I can't see a thing.
Then everything is pink.
I can hear the angels sing.

The roar of those jet engines.
Is music to my ears.
Streaks of black run down my face.
These are happy tears.

Now I see the sky above.
It's filled with clouds dark and black.
The rain drops behind them fall.
Now there's no turning back.

The rains come down the fires drown.
I'm soaked down to my skin.
Here comes another wave.
I'm dancing here again.

As I start to clean my land.
The floods surely will come.
I fill so many sandbags now.
That my strong arms feel numb.

The fires quenched.
The seasons change.
It's cold and wet outside.
Here comes some more weather.
To take me for a ride.

Time Zones

A way too many time zones.
Between you and me.
But I just have to close my eyes.
For your face to see.

The beauty in my sunshine.
The sweetness in my dreams.
As long as I have memories.
You are closer that it seems.

It was only yesterday.
That my eyes were filled with you.
Now you float inside my head.
Filling up that view.

Remorse

Sometimes I feel bad.
For things from the past.
But then I use perspective.
And those feelings never last.

I was young or something else.
The end always had a reason.
The time or the place.
Maybe even 'twas the season.

As I think it through.
As I put it on the shelf.
The end game always is.
I forgive myself.

Nostalgia

Many years and many things.
I have left behind.
Sometimes when I'm all alone.
They begin to cross my mind.

People that I used to know.
Places that I've been,
It may be an old flame.
My old "remember when?"

It could be a pet or a car.
That I might pass on some street.
Or a smell or taste.
That can bring a tasty treat.

The flower that my grandma wore.
In her beautiful graying hair.
Sometimes I pass a garden.
And I see them growing there.

It just may be a broken thing.
That someone threw away.
All of these things are in my head.
And I'm just glad they stay.

Tempo

Lovers love in tempo.
Lovers love in time.
Lovers will get married too.
And that is such a crime.

For that brings the hardships.
The reality of life.
For every lover's husband.
And every lover's wife.

What used to be a lot of fun.
Is now responsibility.
It takes all the fun away.
And now you have to do you see?

The tempo is all shattered now.
With a tiny screaming child.
You have to be tame.
Where once you used to be wild.

I've Been To Heaven

I've been to heaven.
Where they know my face.
Where there's so much love.
And there's so much grace.

Where embraces are many.
With tears of much joy.
Where hate is not known.
And you can never employ.

I've seen the face.
Of my savior himself.
This is the place.
With no one on shelf.

Where no one is loved.
More than another.
Where everyone.
Is my sister and brother.

But the streets are not paved.
In silver nor gold.
Those things are earthly.
Nothing is bought here, nothing is sold.

The only gold here.
That you might feel.
Is in every heart.
And that gold is real.

Flowers bloom.
There's no notice of time.
Grasses are green.
And there is no crime.

You don't see the crippled.
They just don't exist.
They've all been healed.
And sublimely kissed.

There are no scars.
Other than his.
For he paid for our sins.
This is, the only twist.

Bright/Dark

Bright, Dark.
Into the night.
Or in the morning.
With sun shining bright.

You're on my mind.
You're in my heart.
Every moment.
When my thoughts start.

Be it in dreams.
Or conscious thought.
You are my all.
That, with love I have bought.

You fill my eyes.
My senses explode.
When you are near.
I'm on overload.

I know that it's folly.
That we'll never touch.
But I can still dream.
For I love you so much.

Wander

Tell me where you wander.
In your dreams at night.
Do you do the past?
Or the future you find right?

Do you climb the tallest trees.
Like you did as a child?
Or maybe let it all go.
Maybe get a little wild?

Take a run through a meadow.
With a dog you dearly love.
Or confront some dark demon.
By giving it a shove?

Do you even think of me?
Do you dream of kisses by the sea?
When just two young kids we were.
With a love to never be.

Dream

This is my dream.
That I'll never share.
Some you might call.
My personal, nightmare.

For, while I am sleeping.
I am awake.
In your deepest dream.
Where you always forsake.

You give other lovers.
All of your time.
You push me away.
For me, no sublime.

"Go get me a drink."
While you're holding hands.
With some other guy.
On ocean, sprayed sands.

The smell of the oceans.
Of the salty sea.
Is all that you share.
With the likes of me.

And when this one dumps you.
You'll seek my arms.
Like all those before him.
After they've, sampled your charms.

I know that you love me.
But not in the same way.
I'm just your spotter.
When your skies turn gray.

I no longer can do this.
So I'm leaving town.
I can no longer be used.
When you get thrown down.

It's all or nothing.
My heart just can't do.
For it is the one.
Who's love is true.

So when the next one.
Throws you aside?
I'll no longer be here.
To take that ride.

But if you ever.
See your way clear?
If you find that you love me?
I'll be right here.

To hold you and be there.
For the rest of our days.
For mine is true love.
Forever, always.

Impromptu

I saw you today.
And I wanted to.
Make you my friend.
But I don't do, impromptu.

What would I say?
To one such as you?
I get tongue tied.
When you come into view.

If I approached?
What would ensue?
Would I be a fool?
What would you do?

I guess it don't matter.
Because one thing is true.
I'm not off the cuff.
I don't do, im-promptu.

Time

Time is but a concept.
And it's human made.
Today I've got too much of it.
So I'm sitting in the shade.

When I have to be somewhere.
And traffic's standing still?
I watch the seconds tick away.
While thumping on the wheel.

But while I'm sitting on the couch.
And my lady lags behind?
The seconds tick away so fast.
It drives me from my mind.

We are always late to things.
Because of her extra care.
She can spend an hour.
Just choosing under wear.

A groom stands at the altar
Waiting for his bride.
The music stopped long again.
He feels sick inside.

It's only been five minutes.
Since the music stopped.
But to him it seems like hours.
Since his poor heart dropped.

The guests just don't see it.
To them it's nothing bad.
To the father of the bride.
There is no time to be had.

It's the same situation.
The same time and same place.
To the infant in its stroller.
Time really has no pace.

It's all in the perception.
The way we see it go.
Flying by untethered.
Or moving way too slow.

Instant

I need gratification
And I need it right now!
I want it in an instant.
I really don't care how!

It's all about me, you know!
I'm the king right here.
Bring to me my wants and needs.
Can I make it any more clear?

I am the little infant child.
And I make all the noise.
You will cater to my wishes.
Because I bring you love and joys

Shallow

Shallow are the seas
Near the siren's shores.
Many are the ships.
That sail there never more

Shallow are the graves.
Which hold the lovers heart.
Deep are emotions.
When those lovers have to part.

Shallow are the pools.
Where the little children wade.
Shallow are the ones that use.
Then stab you with their blade.

Shallow are the pools of blood.
That can end your life.
Deeper are the feelings.
That fill some hearts with strife.

No Time For Anything

She has no time for anything.
She gives it all away.
If someone needs her help.
She shows up every day.

She never had a lover.
"No time." Was her excuse.
She was in love once you know.
But then he turned her lose.

She had time for everyone.
Except when it came to him.
Now in her dreams each night.
Her love life's looking slim.

One day she will look around.
In the mirror she will find.
An old woman staring back.
How could she be so blind?

Yesterday she saw that man.
Who once had stole her heart.
She sighed when he waved to her.
It tore her dreams apart.

He was walking arm in arm.
With a woman and some kids.
They really did look happy.
She had only "Wish I dids."

Sleep With One Eye Open

Tonight I sleep with one eye open.
As the fires are fanned by the wind.
Wildfires don't give one damn.
They are nobody's friend.

As the fires blaze unhindered.
I listen to the demons wail.
It sounds as if they're women.
Much more ruthless than the male.

As I watch I see the red glowing.
With the orange and the red flame.
I look to the sky for clouds.
There are not, for me to claim.

As I stand with my arms lifted.
To feel the winds beneath my wings.
The embers seem like mighty beasts.
Some most wonderful, hideous things.

The flames as the tempest shifts.
Begin to move my way.
I spread my wings and take to flight.
They'll not consume me today.

I fly along the ridges.
To my cave over hill.
And land and stand and watch.
The flames provide me such a thrill.

For, I am the dragon.
Who watches over this land.
And you'd have to be me.
To come to understand.

The reason I bring the fires on.
With my unholy breath.
Is to bring life back again.
After the living's death.

Fire clears the dry brown brush.
So the rain can bring the plants.
Am I an Angel or a demon?
As I do my flaming dance?

Spiders

Spiders have a way to live.
That's not governed by etiquette.
They spin their webs with precision
And they will never quit.

It's their way to dinner time.
And who am I to say?
How a spider should run his life,
Any, other way.

Chains

Chains without shackles.
Chains without locks.
Ain't no way you'll throw me in.
Sittin on these docks.

You once was my master.
Under lock and key.
My heart was bound and gagged.
You brought me misery.

But now I cast these chains off.
And once again I'm free!
They're now wrapped around your neck.
At the bottom of the sea.

The Beast Within

There's a beast within my soul.
That anger will release.
The more I get upset.
The more it will increase.

I have a low tolerance.
For gross stupidity.
And when I encounter it.
The beast is released, in me,

If I try to reason.
With someone that won't listen.
I'm pretty laid back.
But soon my brow will glisten.

If they start to calling names?
My beast there inside.
Balls his fists in fits of rage.
You better not hurt my pride.

Dodge

I've always been a fan of Dodge.
Practically all my life.
I love the way they perform.
And so does my wife.

69 Superbee.
Was my favorite one.
383 and four on the floor.
Horsepower by the ton.

Once a friend told me.
He had followed me to town.
But he couldn't catch me.
And he had to power down.

When he caught up to my car.
At a red stoplight.
He saw my wife was driving.
For him, most unusual sight.

There were times my friends and I.
Would travel three abreast.
Driving at one hundred and ten.
Those times were the best.

And now at 72.
I still love to drive,
We still drive those Dodge cars.
But we keep it under, 95.

Hemis are best I say.
That's why we own two.
And do my best to keep them up.
Because that's the right thing to do.

Drip

Drip drip drip…
Drop.
I'm trying to sleep.
And it won't stop.

I get up and bend.
I turn the handle.
What happens next?
A homeowner's scandal.

I turn it as far.
As it will go.
The frequency increases.
Fatster, not slow.

I go into my tools shed.
Bleary, teary eyed.
I'm so weak from tired
It's been a long time since I cried.

I open up my plumbing box.
I take a look inside.
If I connect this to that?
And use it from the side…

I can disconnect the hose.
And use it for plug.
I grab my roll of Teflon tape.
And it rolls across the rug.

I gather up the ribboned mess.
And stumble to the sink.
I open up the doors.
And I try my best to think.

I forgot the wrenches.
In my stupor and I sigh.
I don't have to wonder.
I know exactly why.

I put down the things I brought.
And stumble back again.
I trip over my old tool box.
(Is cussing loud a sin?)

My neighbor comes a rushing.
With his shotgun is his hands.
Trips and it goes off.
There go his, "best for me" plans.

His shot takes out the main line.
The biggest water source.
I throw up my hands.
This is par for my course.

I look for my cell.
But it's soaked and wet.
My neighbor offers his.
Through remorse and regret.

I phone call the plumber.
And he's laughing til he hurts.
Made some stupid jokes.
About how shotguns shoot in spurts.

It's way past 2 am.
When he shows his smiling face.
He takes out his pen and pad.
$4000.00 to replace.

He puts on a pressure band.
Says he'll come today.
Laughs at his "funny".
Then he drives away.

Crap! I forgot the dripper.
And now it's 4 am.
I send my neighbor packing.
As try now not to swim.

Well… there's my old fishing boat.
Under a cover right outside.
I grab a couple of sleeping bags.
Then I settle down inside.

My watch says it's 5am.
I send my boss a text.
I still have my neighbor's cell.
So my boss is perplexed.

By the time I call and explain.
It's 5:30 now.
I finally get to some needed sleep,

Then I hear a whack and pow!
The plumber has arrived to work.
So I give to him my key.
As he puts on his silly smirk.

I tell him bout the the drippy leak.
And says he'll take a look.
Then out comes one more time.
His estimation book.

I tell him to hell with cost.
Just to get it fixed.
Then I go to a cheap hotel.
Right there and in betwixed.

It's too damned near the freeway.
Then I hear the drip drip drop.
That's when exhaustion takes me down.
I sleep for ten nonstop.

Castle

She said she wanted a life in a castle.
So he built it from the ground up to the sky.
He broke so many bones in the process.
But she never shed a tear drop from her eye.

She wanted a throne and some subjects.
So he built for them a town in which to live.
When he went to find her some good people.
He found there was no more for him to give.

Her reputation had preceded.
And the way she treated him was renown.
No one wanted to come along to live.
In the perfect under castle little town.

Randy Hayes

Randy Hayes is a new poet, having been writing for well over 50 years. He writes about things of everyday life, love, kittens and anything else that might enter his mind on any given day or night. Raised in Southern California, in Ventura County. He spent his younger years climbing the hills along Ventura Ave. In his teen years he could be found riding motorcycles or hunting in the area around Ojai California. His hobbies have always been writing, cars and motorcycles. He still can be found fishing or target shooting in the high desert of California.